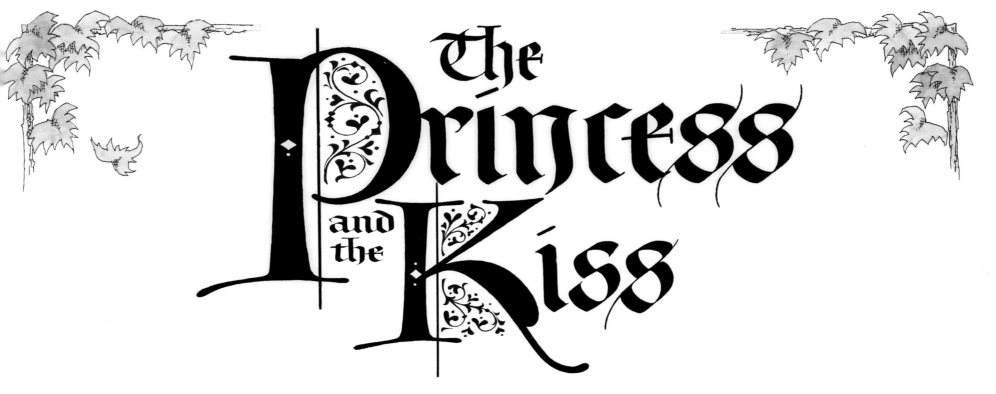

The Princess and the Kiss

By Jennie Bishop

Layout design by John Silvey

Illustrated by Preston McDaniels

WARNER
Press

Text © 1999 by Jennie Bishop.   Illustrations © 1999 Warner Press.

Scripture marked NIV taken from the HOLY BIBLE: NEW INTERNATIONAL VERSION®. NIV®. Copyright © 1973, 1978, 1984 by International Bible Society. Used by permission of Zondervan Publishing House.

Published by Warner Press, P.O. Box 2499, Anderson, IN 46018

Printed in Singapore.   ISBN 0 87162 868 6

DEDICATION
This book is dedicated to
Vashti and Christianna.
May your kisses be spent to God's glory!

J. B.

Long ago, in a wonderful castle
on a mountain of splendor,
a beautiful princess was born.
her parents were the king and queen
of the mountain and
all the green valley below.

The king and queen loved the little princess even before she was born. On the day she came into the world, the royal couple gave their daughter a very special gift from God—her first kiss. While the princess was growing up, the king and queen kept this precious gift safe in their care.

hen the princess was finally grown, the king and queen
called her to their side.

"We have something very special to give you,"
said the queen.

Up, up, up the royal family went to a secret room in a
tower of the castle. On an elegant table in the center of the
room was the same gift given to the princess long ago ... the kiss.

od gave this gift to you on the day you were born," said the queen, "because He loves you so dearly."

"And now," continued the king, "this kiss is yours to keep . . . or to give away, as you see fit."

The princess stared in amazement. She had never before received such a wonderful present.

"But use wisdom, my daughter," warned the king, "and save your kiss for the man you will marry. Never part with it for the sake of a stranger."

The wise little princess took her father's words to heart and kept the kiss safe in the castle tower. But there were many days when she went to gaze at her precious possession. She wondered how she could ever give it up.

inally there came a day when suitors began to appear, asking for the princess' hand in marriage.

The first man who came to court her was Prince Peacock. "See the great muscles I have, Princess!" he said. "I will always be able to save you from danger. I can run faster and jump higher than any other prince in the world. I am mighty! Marry me, for I am a man among men."

The princess watched Prince Peacock lift heavy boulders and run the length of the castle wall. His strength was impressive, but the wise princess saw that his heart was full of himself. She knew there would be no room for her kiss there.

So the princess sent Prince Peacock away.

The next day, Prince Romance came to visit the princess. He brought dozens of roses and boxes of chocolates. "I can take you to many far-off places, Princess," he said. "We will eat the choicest foods. We will see marvelous sights. Marry me, Princess. Every day will seem like a honeymoon if you are with me."

The princess thought about what Prince Romance had said. It sounded very interesting and exciting, but the wise princess knew that honeymoons and wonderful feelings could not last forever. This prince would soon lose interest in her kiss.

The princess turned Prince Romance politely away.

On the following morning, Prince Treasurechest came to call. He brought gifts of gold, jewels and costly silken robes. "See the presents I have brought you, Princess," said Prince Treasurechest. "You will never lack for fine clothes. Marry me, Princess, for I can give you the best of everything."

Indeed, when the princess saw the beautiful things the prince had brought for her, she did not doubt that he would buy her anything her heart desired. "But with all these riches," she thought, "he does not need my kiss. My kiss will not be special to him."

So the princess sent Prince Treasurechest away, too.

Many men came, one by one, to ask for the princess'
hand in marriage. One by one she turned them all
away. None seemed worthy of her kiss. She began
to doubt that she would ever find a husband.

One night, she spoke with her mother,
the queen, about her fears.

"Mama," the princess asked, "will I ever find a man so special that I will be able to give him my kiss?"

The queen smiled, gazing at the many stars twinkling above in the velvet night.

"Oh, yes, my dear. I think God will bring a husband to you. But, if he does not, the kiss will be yours to treasure forever."

The princess took comfort in that thought, for she knew that God could be trusted, and she cherished the kiss with all that she was.

The next day, a common man came to the castle. He asked to see the princess. The man was dressed in farmers' clothes and did not look like the suitors who had lately come to call. Strong and handsome, his hands were rough from working in the king's fields, and his face was tanned from the sun.

"Who is he?" the servants wondered as he was led through the castle.

The man was taken to the royal garden where the princess and her parents were walking among the rosebushes.

The farmer bowed humbly, and addressed the king and queen.
"May I speak with your daughter?" he asked.

The princess' mother and father were surprised. Who was this man?
he seemed common — yet kindness was in his manner.
Nodding slowly, the king and queen moved aside and stood close by.

The man looked into the princess' eyes.

"I have worked in your father's fields for many years. I prayed and
watched and waited for one who could be my wife, yet found no one.
Then one day I saw you walking on the palace lawn. Your beauty was
marvelous, and your purity sparkled like diamonds."

The princess blushed, and her heart began to beat wildly.

"I have little to offer you, Princess," the man said softly. "I have no gold.
I have no means to travel the earth. I am not as strong as many ..."

The farmer stopped, and the princess was afraid he would not continue.
Then he whispered," ... but I do have one very special gift I can give to you."

his is my first kiss, Princess," said the man. "God gave this gift to me on the day I was born. My parents kept it for me until I became a man. I have saved it all my life for you. Would you be my wife?"

The king, the queen, and the princess rejoiced and embraced the humble farmer. Was there any doubt that he was the one the princess had been waiting for? The princess thought her heart would burst with joy!

"Yes!" she cried. "Oh, yes, with all my heart!"

On the day of their wedding, the princess and her husband were dressed in magnificent clothes and stood before the altar in the royal church, where all the lords and ladies of the kingdom had gathered for the celebration. There, with the sun streaming through the windows, they exchanged their kisses, and God and all the kingdom sang for happiness.

The prince and princess lived happily ever after. Soon God gave them a child of their very own. And on the day of the precious baby's birth, the wise prince and princess received for their child a very special gift from God....

"Love . . . comes from a pure heart and a good conscience and a sincere faith."

1 TIMOTHY 1:5 NIV